COMPUTERS AT YOUR SERVICE

PRENTICE-HALL, INC., ENGLEWOOD CLIFFS, N. J.

COMPUTERS
AT YOUR SERVICE

BERNICE KOHN

illustrated by ALIKI

also by Bernice Kohn *Our Tiny Servants: Molds and Yeasts*
illustrated by John Kaufmann

J 53216

for David, my private computer

The author is grateful to
R. Barry Borden, Research Assistant,
University of Pennsylvania Computer Center,
who was kind enough to check the manuscript.

CONTENTS

1

WHAT IS

A COMPUTER?

At Cape Canaveral, Florida, a group of scientists wait tensely near a launching pad. A giant rocket stands ready for flight. It will launch a new satellite. The countdown ends. There is a flash and a roar. The rocket moves skyward. Up and up it goes.

Will the rocket take the right path? Will the satellite be placed in orbit?

In the control room, a few men push buttons and turn dials on the front of big machines. Suddenly, they send up a cheer. The machines have just given the men the answer they wanted to hear. The satellite is in orbit. The launching has been a success.

The president of a large company wants to know how many motors his factories made that day. The office is in Chicago but the factories are scattered all over the United States. The president pushes a button on his

desk. Within one second he knows exactly how many motors were made in each factory. He can also find out, just as quickly, how many motors were sold and how many remain in each factory's stockroom.

A man walks into an airline office in New York. He wants to buy two tickets on the next plane to Boston. The clerk pushes a button behind the counter. A moment later she tells the man that there is only one seat left on the Boston flight. Just then a red light flashes. The clerk smiles and says, "You are lucky, sir. Someone has just returned a ticket. Now I can let you have two."

Where did all these speedy answers come from? They came from *computers* (say: com-PEW-ters). The word computer comes from a Latin word which means to count.

A computer is really a very special kind of counting machine. It can do arithmetic problems faster than any person alive. By means of electrical circuits it can find the answer to a very difficult and lengthy problem in a few seconds.

Some arithmetic is very, very complicated. But, luckily, the most difficult problem can be broken down into a large number of simple addition and subtraction examples. The only thing wrong with this method is that it might take years—even centuries—to do so many examples with a pencil and paper.

But watch a computer do it! There is a whir, a click, a flash of lights as the computer changes the problem to thousands of tiny examples. *Whiz-z-z* out comes the answer—not in centuries, not in years, but in seconds!

A computer can "remember" information you give it. It stores the information in its "memory" until it is needed. When you are ready to solve a problem, you can get the computer to sort through its stored facts and use only the proper ones. It works the problem with lightning speed. Then it checks its work to make sure there are no errors!

There are different kinds of computers. Some do only one job over and over again. These are **special-purpose** computers. One special-purpose computer automatically controls the movements of anti-aircraft cannon. It was built for this purpose alone, and cannot do anything else.

But there are some computers that can do many different jobs. They are called **general-purpose** computers. These are the "big brains" that solve the most difficult problems of science. They answer questions about rockets and planes, bridges and ships—long before these things are even built.

The designer of a ship, for example, might feed a general-purpose computer such facts as the size and weight of the ship, the kind of metal to be used, the shape of the sides, and the type of engines that will move it. The computer then quickly figures out how fast the ship will go, how it will behave in the water, and what troubles it may have. On the basis of what the computer reports,

plans may be changed. In this way, trouble is not built in. It is corrected before it happens!

Computers help our space program, our armed forces, our business and industry. They are powerful tools which will help to change our lives and the world around us.   13

2

SIMPLE ARITHMETIC

A computer is a wizard at arithmetic. It can solve problems in a flash. It even has a memory.

The computer sounds very intelligent, doesn't it? Well, it *can* solve difficult problems—but it solves them in a very simple way. All that a computer can really *do* is answer "yes" or "no." And each astonishing task that it performs is a result of a series of these simple answers.

When you flip a wall switch, the light goes on. Flip it again and the light goes off. When the switch is on, electrical current flows through the wires. When the switch is off, so is the current.

Most wall switches have "on" and "off" printed on them. They *could* say "yes" and "no" instead.

A computer says "yes" and "no" with numbers. And since "yes" and "no" are the only two things it can say, 14 a computer uses only two numbers.

You do arithmetic with ten numbers: 0-1-2-3-4-5-6-7-8-9. This is called the *decimal system. Deci-* means 10.

The decimal system came into use because we have ten fingers. Early man counted on his fingers. When he got to the end of his fingers, he had to start over. The word *digit* (say: DIJ-it), which is another name for number, comes from a Latin word meaning finger or toe.

A computer doesn't count on its fingers. It has none. It uses the number 0 to say off, or no. It uses the number 1 to say on, or yes. These are the only two numbers a computer uses. This is called the *binary* (say: BY-nary) system. *Bi-* means 2.

People who use the binary system have put together the two words **bi**nary and **di**g**it** and formed the word **bit.** A bit is a binary number.

Let's see how this binary arithmetic works. In the decimal system, 9 is our highest single number. When we add two numbers, if the sum is larger than 9, we must carry. In the example

$$\begin{array}{r} 4 \\ +6 \\ \hline 10 \end{array}$$

we say to ourselves, $4+6=10$.

Then we put down the 0 and carry the 1 to the next column.

In the binary system, the highest number is 1. When we add two binary numbers, if the sum is larger than 1, we put down 0 and carry the 1 to the next column.

Here are four binary sums. The first two have no carried numbers at all. The third example has one carried number. The fourth example has two.

0	0	1	11
+0	+1	+1	+01
0	1	10	100

The first two examples are just like ordinary arithmetic. But in the third one, when we add 1 and 1, we get an answer higher than 1. However, there *is* no binary digit (or bit) higher than 1. Therefore, we put down 0 and carry the 1 to the next column.

In the last example we say 1 and 1 is more than 1. So we put down 0 and carry 1 to the next column. Now we have to add 0 and 1 plus the 1 we carried. This, again, adds up to more than 1. So once more we put down 0 and carry 1 to the next column.

It may seem strange to you to do arithmetic with only two numbers. Actually, many different number systems have been used. The ancient Mayans had twenty numbers and the Babylonians sixty. The Australian aborigines used two—the binary system!

Decimal	0	1	2	3	4	5	6	7	8	9	10
Binary	0	1	10	11	100	101	110	111	1000	1001	1010

Let's change 39 to a binary number. Divide 39 by 2. Then divide your answer by 2. Then divide *that* answer by 2. Keep going. Divide every answer by 2 until you can't divide any more. Keep the remainders in a column. Like this:

$$
\begin{array}{r}
1 \qquad\quad \text{remainder } 0 \\
2\overline{)\,2} \qquad\quad \text{remainder } 0 \\
2\overline{)\,4} \qquad\quad \text{remainder } 1 \\
2\overline{)\,9} \qquad\quad \text{remainder } 1 \\
2\overline{)\,19} \qquad\quad \text{remainder } 1 \\
2\overline{)\,39}
\end{array}
$$

start here ↑

To get the answer, we take the *last* answer to the division examples—1—and then all the remainders in order, going *down* the column. So 39 in binary numbers is 100111.

Here is another way to do it. Instead of calling the number columns units, tens, hundreds, thousands, as in decimal arithmetic, we do it this way: the first column on the right is units, or ones. Each time you move over a column to the left, you multiply by 2. So the columns are:

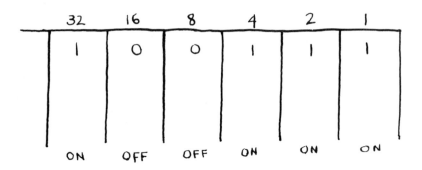

Now we say, "Is there a 32 in 39?" There is one, so we put a 1 in the 32 column. 32 from 39 leaves a remainder of 7. Is there a 16 in 7? No, so we put 0 in the 16 column. Is there an 8 in 7? No, so we put 0 in the 8 column. Is there a 4 in 7? Yes, there is. We put a 1 in the 4 column and now we have a remainder of 3. And there is a 2 and a 1 in 3, so we put a 1 in each of those columns. Now let's check. Add 32, 0, 0, 4, 2, 1. Did you get 39?

When you feed the number 39 into a computer it means: in the first 6 wires—current on, current off, current off, current on, current on, current on.

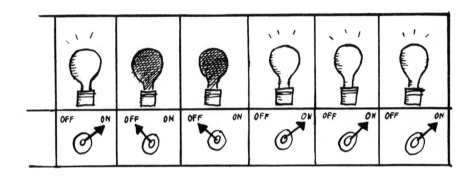

Now we know how a computer gets instructions. Let's see what it does with them.

3

BIG BRAINS

We often hear computers called "electronic brains." Is a computer a "brain"? Can a machine think? Let's find out how a computer works and see just how much "thinking" it can do.

A computer has five main parts. The first part is called the *input*. Input means the place where you *put in* or *feed* information to the machine. Information can be fed to the computer in a number of ways. It can be typed directly on a keyboard, or switches may be flipped. Or, the machine may be fed magnetic tape, punched paper tape, or punched cards.

The second part of the computer is the *control* unit. Here the machine carries out the instructions that you have given it. The instructions for a computer are called a *program*. The person who plans the instructions is called the *programmer*.

3 The third part of the computer is the memory, or *storage* unit. Information fed to the computer can be used at once, or stored until needed. It can be used once and then "forgotten." Or, it can remain in storage and be used over and over again. It can also be replaced by new information at any time.

Now we come to the main "works" of the computer. This is the arithmetic or *processing* unit. It is here that the machine really does its work. The processing unit can add, subtract, multiply, divide, and compare numbers—all at lightning speed.

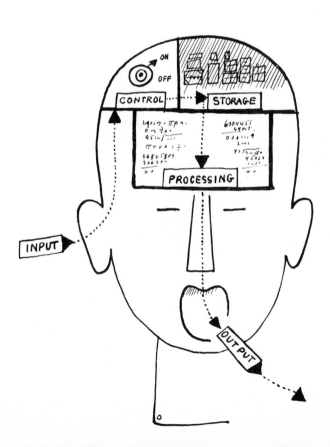

The answer to the problem wouldn't help us if we didn't know what it was. We find out through the *output*. The output is the part of a computer that gives us information. Sometimes it prints automatically on an electric typewriter. Or, it may record information on magnetic tape or punch it into paper tape or cards.

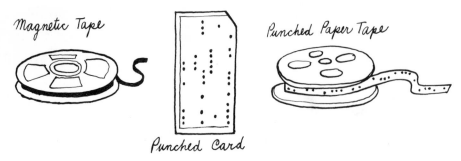

Magnetic Tape

Punched Card

Punched Paper Tape

Let's see how the five parts of the computer work for us when we have a problem to solve.

Luckily, we don't have to speak "computer language." We can feed information into the computer in decimal numbers or in words. The computer translates them into bits and does its work. Then it changes its answer back into numbers or words we can understand.

When we feed a punched card or tape into the machine, there are tiny metal fingers that feel for the holes. Wherever there is a hole, an electrical current flows. This is the same as saying "yes," and the bit 1 appears. Where there is no hole, there is no current. This is "no"—or 0.

When the programmer punches holes or magnetizes spots on tape, he gives the machine information that it can use. But—and this is very important—the computer can only do what the programmer tells it to do.

The program might say, "When you get the first four numbers, add them together. Take the sum and divide it by 17. When you get that answer, multiply it by 5,690. Then add the next number you receive and subtract the one after that. When you get the answer, remember it while you do the next three examples. Then add answer number 1 to answer number 4 and tell me what it is."

The answer will be whisked out almost before you can blink your eyes. But the computer does exactly what it is told to do. If the programmer makes a mistake, so will the machine!

The storage unit of a computer may be a *magnetic core*, a *magnetic drum* or a *magnetic disk*. Even though there are three kinds of storage unit, they all begin with the word "magnetic." This is because they all work by means of a magnetized spot to show current or no current—our old friends 1 and 0 again.

Storage is arranged something like a group of mail boxes in a post office. Each box has a special number, called an *address*. When the programmer puts new information into an address, he wipes out whatever was in it before. But if he **takes** information from an address, it is not wiped out. It can be used as often as needed.

To get some idea of a computer's speed, let's take just one model. You can put in 62,500 numbers in one second. The arithmetic is done in **millionths of a second.** The magnetic disk storage can remember 16,000 different instructions. The answers are automatically printed at a rate of 1285 long lines every minute! A fast typist can type about 10 such lines a minute.

Computers are certainly wonderful machines—but are they "brains"? Do they think?

The *New York Times* once printed a cartoon which showed a great big computer. The man in charge of it was sitting in front of the controls reading a book. He looked very surprised to see the computer spinning out a strip of printed tape which said, "May I borrow it after you finish?"

This is a funny joke. But it *is* a joke because it's impossible. A computer can only do what it is told to do. It has no brain. It can't think. Men must do the thinking for the computer!

4

HOW IT ALL BEGAN

The electronic computer is a very new invention. But many things led up to it.

A great French mathematician named *Pascal* (say: pass-KAL) invented an adding machine way back in 1642. Another mathematician, *Leibnitz* (say: LIBE-nits), improved this machine in 1672. It could now multiply and divide as well as add.

Gottfried Wilhelm Leibnitz

25

Then, almost two centuries later, an Englishman, Charles Babbage, worked out the idea of a real computer. But Babbage was too far ahead of his time. His idea was excellent, but it just wasn't possible to get the kinds of machine parts he needed. He never built his computer.

In the 1870's another Englishman, Lord Kelvin, built a machine to predict the tides. Lord Kelvin called his invention an *harmonic analyzer*—but it was really a kind of computer. It was a successful machine. It was used in many parts of the world up until about fifty years ago.

Over the years, there were many improvements in "counting machines." In the 1930's Dr. Vannevar Bush and a group of students at the Massachusetts Institute of Technology built the first modern computer. In 1943, a much improved model was built at Harvard University. It was called *Mark I*.

These were all important steps—but they were just steps. The first electronic "big brain" came from the University of Pennsylvania in 1946. Its real name was the *Electronic Numerical Integrator and Calculator*. But nobody felt like saying all that! Someone thought of using the first letter of each word to make *Eniac*—and *Eniac* it was, from then on.

Since all computers have long, hard names, it became very popular to make up a nickname from the initials. Almost every computer you read about will have such a pet name.

Eniac was built especially to help the U. S. Army Ordnance people in World War II. They found many new ways to build better guns and cannon—but every new weapon had to have a complicated set of firing instructions. It took a small army of mathematicians to work them out—and as soon as they had finished, there was another new weapon. Then the mathematicians started all over again. It just took too long. There was no time to spare.

When *Eniac* came along, the problem was solved. As soon as there was a new weapon a couple of operators fed some punched cards into the machine. *Whiz*—out came the instructions! *Eniac* did 5,000 additions a second. It took two weeks of programming work and two hours at the machine to solve a problem that would have taken 100 engineers a whole year to do!

Eniac was soon followed by a whole family of giants. Some of their names are *Univac, Erma, Rez, Sage, Norc, Whirlwind, Fosdic, Bizmac,* and *Audrey*. We shall get to know some of them quite well a little later.

The first electronic computers filled up a good-sized room. *Eniac* had 500,000 soldered connections and 18,000 vacuum tubes. (A radio has about 6 tubes.) As if that weren't enough, there was another room full of air conditioners. Without them, the *first* roomful of machinery would have melted in its own great heat.

But when tiny *transistors* were invented to replace

Transistor magnified twice in size

tubes, the size of computers shrank. Printed circuits instead of miles of wire also helped. There are many small-sized computers now. One of them, *Recomp II*, is the size of a large suitcase. It weighs about two hundred pounds. This computer can be carried by two men and doesn't need air conditioning at all.

In spite of *Recomp's* small size, it can do a big job. Midget computers of this type have become popular in many offices and factories.

The most modern computers work about fifty times as fast as *Eniac* did. They can do 250,000 additions a second. Wouldn't you like to have a computer to do your homework?

5

COMPUTERS
IN THE SPACE RACE

On October 4, 1957, *Sputnik I* was put into orbit around the earth. So began a new era—the start of man's exploration in space. So also began the IBM Space Computing Center.

Programmers at this center have worked out a system to predict the path that every U. S. satellite will take. It has been widely used by the National Aeronautics and Space Administration (NASA).

Very valuable experiments have been made with satellites. They would all have been impossible if the exact orbits of the satellites were not known.

There is an *IBM 709* computer at Cape Canaveral, Florida. In one second, this computer can do over 40,000 additions and subtractions. Or, it can do 5,000 multiplications and divisions of 10 digit numbers!

The computer predicts the orbit of the satellite in advance. As soon as the rocket is fired, the 709 follows its course. Ten times every second it sends information to the safety officer. This gives him a chance to destroy the rocket in case anything has gone wrong and there is danger of an accident.

As the computer follows the satellite's path, all information on it is sent at once to the Space Computing Center in Washington, D.C. The scientists there can then figure out many days in advance where the satellite will be and what its speed will be at every minute.

To do this, they store over 40,000 computer instructions on magnetic tape. As it follows these instructions, the 709 may solve as many as five million problems a day.

Many new discoveries have been made possible by the computer's fast and accurate work.

Dr. James Van Allen discovered a large area in space where there are very strong and dangerous rays. It has been named the *Van Allen radiation belt*. This knowledge is very important to space crews. Without it, perhaps, the men would be killed by the deadly rays.

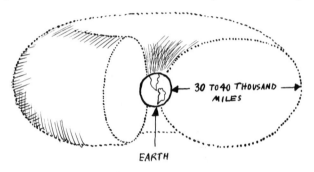

30 TO 40 THOUSAND MILES

EARTH

When the orbit of *Vanguard I* was studied, new discoveries were made about the shape of the earth. It was found to be slightly pear-shaped.

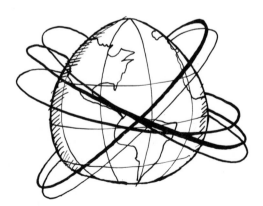

Tiros (Television Infrared Observation Satellites) study weather conditions. They measure the clouds that cover the earth. They also tell us the temperature of the earth and clouds and the amount of radiation from the sun.

Tiros III, which was sent up in 1961, supplies weather-watchers with information on storms and hurricanes. This early warning system saves many lives and a great deal of property. It gives people a chance to prepare for a dangerous storm—and to get away from islands or sea-coasts that might be flooded.

A computer figures out the exact position of *Tiros* as it spins around the earth. Without this information no measurements could be made.

The most exciting of NASA's projects is *Project Mercury*. This is the program which plans manned space flights. Computers work on every step of this project. They work out the orbit and follow the man through every moment of the flight. Then they plan when and how to bring the capsule safely back to earth.

Project Echo is a first step to set up space stations. The stations will be able to send signals, voice and television. The Echo satellite is an aluminum-covered ball that measures one hundred feet across. Two-way radio signals are bounced off it while it is in orbit 1,000 miles up! Again, computers do all the arithmetic.

Rockets and satellites move with such great speed that no mathematician could possibly solve problems fast enough to follow the flight. By the time a person found the answer it would no longer be of use. The rocket would be hundreds of miles away.

Only a computer can do arithmetic fast enough to keep up with a rocket. Surely, without computers, man could not have entered space.

6

ERMA AND AUDREY

Erma's full name is *Electronic Recording Machine-Accounting.* She is a banking expert.

Erma was built over a period of five years by the Stanford Research Institute in California. She went to work in 1956 at the Bank of America at San Jose, California. She does all the bookkeeping for the checking accounts of four branch banks. She took over the work of fifty girls!

The checks at *Erma's* bank have a group of black dashes on the back. They are printed in magnetic ink. They tell *Erma* in computer language what she needs to know.

The only thing *Erma* can't do for herself is read the amount of money written on the check. Someone has to do this for her. A clerk punches out the amount of the check on *Erma's* keyboard. He also pushes a button which tells whether the sum of money is to be put into, or taken out of, the account. *Erma* lights up a sign which shows the amount. The clerk checks it to make sure it is right. Then he feeds the check into a slot and *Erma* goes to work.

Suppose the check is for $12.00 and is to be added to someone's account. *Erma* reads her special code on the back of the check and finds that it means 15723884. She knows that 157 is the number of the branch bank and 23884 is the depositor's number. *Erma's* memory tells her that 23884 is Mr. John Jones and that he has $46.00 in the bank.

The processing unit swiftly adds $12.00 to $46.00 and gets $58.00. Almost immediately, this new balance is flashed to the storage unit and the old balance, $46.00, is wiped out.

At the same time that *Erma* is working on John Jones' check, she is also working on four others. She adds and subtracts at the same time and never gets mixed up. Every time she finishes an arithmetic example she checks the work and proves it to make sure there is no error.

At the end of each day, *Erma* runs through everything she has done for the day and sees that all of the information is up to date on reels of magnetic tape and in her main memory.

At the end of the month, a bank statement has to be sent to every one of *Erma's* 38,000 depositors. This shows the depositor each sum of money he put into the bank and each sum he took out. It also shows any service charges the bank may have made and tells exactly how much is left. It used to take fifty girls a whole month to get the statements ready for the mail. Now these girls have been released to take better jobs in the same bank.

When *Erma's* reels of magnetic tape are placed on her high speed printer, a completed statement whizzes out every two and a half seconds. The whole batch of 38,000 is finished in two days!

If you ask your parents to show you a check, you will probably see dashes or numbers printed on it in magnetic ink. *Erma's* children and grandchildren are now at work in banks all over the country.

Another computer girl you might like to meet is *Audrey*. *Audrey* isn't really finished yet. She is still "in the works"—but interesting just the same.

Audrey is the invention of the Bell Telephone Laboratories and she understands the human voice! So far, she doesn't understand many words, but she is fine with numbers. When any number from one to ten is spoken into an ordinary telephone mouthpiece, *Audrey* shows that she has understood. She flashes the number on a lighted sign.

Engineers hope that some day we will be able to make long distance telephone calls without any help at all from a live operator. We will tell the number to *Audrey*, and she will make the connection automatically.

She may also be able to carry on a conversation. Although she doesn't speak well as yet, she can recognize and repeat a number of sounds. Her voice is a bit spooky —but it can be understood.

In the future, you may call a store to order some groceries. The conversation will be something like this:

> *Voice:* Good morning. May I help you?
> You: Yes, please. I would like to have a package of Crunchums.
> *Voice:* I'm very sorry but we don't have any

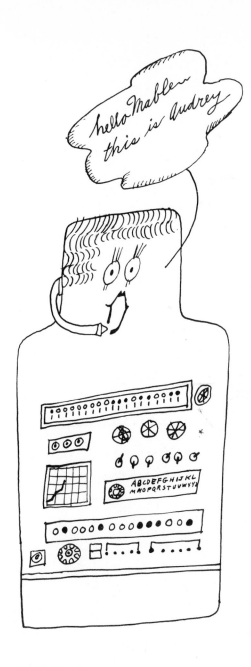

Crunchums. Will you take Munchums instead?

You: Yes, that will be fine.

Voice: Do you want the super-large package, or the extra-giant package?

You: I'll have the super-large size, please.

Voice: Thank you for your order. It will be delivered in one hour.

But—won't you be surprised to find out that the grocer was busy waiting on customers all the time you were on the phone and that, you had your whole conversation with a computer!

7

SAGE AND TALOS

Sage is the big, big computer that helps to guard our country against enemy attack in case of war.

Sage can spot any plane or missile that approaches our shores. He can report both the location and the speed of an object he tracks. *Sage* is so watchful, that he sometimes gets excited when a flock of birds goes by!

A group of Air Force men sit in a large room with many television screens. As soon as a flying object is spotted, it appears on the screens. *Sage* immediately figures out the direction of the plane, its height, and its speed.

The Air Force men have rows of push buttons with which they can ask questions. If they think the plane is a commercial one, they ask *Sage*.

Sage has in his memory complete information about every plane that is expected in the area that day. He may flash back that the 3:00 P.M. plane from Boston to Chicago was ten minutes late leaving the airport. It should be on the television screens just at that moment. The Air Force people check until they are sure, then they tell *Sage*. From then on, the plane is marked with an *F* for friend as it moves across the screens.

So far, there have been only friends. But every once in awhile, *Sage* is tested in a war game. Special target planes are sent up for *Sage* to find. And he finds them at once, even though they are hundreds of miles away. He immediately decides what path the planes will take and how best to fight them.

If it seems to be a job for fighter planes, *Sage* decides which airport they should leave from and how many planes are needed. If a guided missile is the best thing to use, *Sage* says so. He watches every move in the battle, and changes his orders whenever he thinks it best.

Each time *Sage* makes a new plan, it is sent to the fighter pilots by radio. The pilots have only to think of the battle. *Sage* navigates the plane automatically. He also knows if the plane is about to run out of fuel. If it is, *Sage* orders it to return to the ground, and sends up another plane instead.

In time, the entire United States will be covered by *Sage* defense posts. If any enemy plane should try to enter our country, it would get a very speedy "welcome" from our Air Force—with the help of *Sage*.

One of *Sage's* close pals is *Talos*. *Talos* automatically sends up missiles to fight enemy planes.

If an enemy craft should come into range, *Talos* would spot it, track it, and rocket off a missile to hit it. This whole job is controlled by the computer—no human help is needed to launch the rocket.

As soon as *Talos* has picked the proper missile for the job, he opens the heavy doors of the storage room. Then the automatic launcher swings around, and sends a cart down a track to the open door. The missile is automatically loaded onto the cart and returned to the launcher. As soon as it is fastened in place, it is swung into position. At the proper moment, the booster rocket is fired—also by *Talos*.

Of course we all hope that our country will never, never be at war. But *should* war come, we will all feel safer to have those two great fighters on the job—*Sage* and *Talos*.

8

IS THIS SEAT TAKEN?

Computers are used every day in airline ticket offices. They make sure that there will be a seat for everyone who buys a ticket.

Until computers came along, if you wanted to buy a plane ticket, you called the airline office and placed your order. The agent took your telephone number, and said that he would call you back in several hours.

He then called or wired a central office to find out how many seats were left on the flight. Sometimes, you got the bad news that there was no space left at all. But by then it was so late, that even if you got a reservation on another plane, you couldn't get to your appointment on time.

That kind of delay doesn't happen any more, thanks to the computer reservation system.

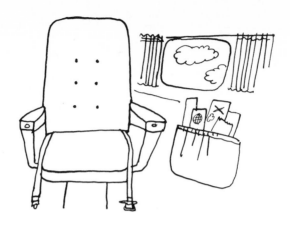

If you go into an airline office, don't look around for a big computer. The computer is far away—perhaps in another city. You *will* see an *agent set*—something that looks a bit like an adding machine. Let's see how it works.

Suppose you decide to travel from Chicago to New York. There are forty-four seats on the plane you want to take. However, not all of the seats will be sold in Chicago. Many passengers will come from other cities to get the New York plane in Chicago. Tickets for the flight will be on sale in cities all over the United States.

When you are ready to buy your ticket, you call the airline office in your city. You tell the agent that you want one seat on Flight 234 on March 28. The agent then turns to his agent set. He presses buttons which show the flight number (234), the city you want to leave from (Chicago), the number of seats you want (1), the date (3-28), and a button marked *sell*. (If you wanted to *cancel* a reservation, he would push the cancel button instead of the sell button.)

All of this information is immediately flashed to the company's central computer. Within three seconds, a flash of lights on the agent set says either that there is a seat for you or there is not. If the plane is filled, the agent can immediately ask for space on another flight in the same way.

As soon as your agent pushes his sell button, the computer automatically subtracts that seat from the number that are left. If a ticket is cancelled, the computer immediately adds it to the total number. The total number of seats for sale is always correct and always right up to the minute.

The airline computer also performs another important service for the air traveler.

Have you ever gone to meet a plane at the airport only to find that it was expected to be two hours late? Or, worse yet, that it had arrived early and your favorite uncle got tired of waiting and went off on a bus? Small airports very often did not have the latest news of delays or helping tail winds.

Now, if you call the airline to check on an arrival time, the agent can ask the computer. He presses the proper button on his agent set and gets a prompt answer. The central computer knows where the plane is and can tell at any moment whether it is on time or late.

Computers have done a great deal to make air travel easy and pleasant. Some day they may do a great deal more. Who knows? The plane of tomorrow might even have a computer for a pilot!

9

LOOK, MA —
NO HANDS!

One of the most exciting jobs that computers have been programmed to do is to run a factory—completely automatically.

The idea of an automatic factory is not really new. In 1784, Oliver Evans built an automatic grain mill near Philadelphia. Although it was considered a marvel at the time, no one would be very much impressed today. The mill was automatic because it had a series of moving belts. The grain was moved by means of these belts to the grinders. After it had been ground, the grain was moved on belts again to be bagged. Finally, belts carried the bags of grain to the shipping area.

What a difference between Oliver Evans' mill and today's automatic factory! We used to think that things were automatic if we could make them work by pushing a button. Now, we don't even have to push the button! The computer does it for us.

Many industries have factories, or portions of factories, that are run by computers. Among them are steel, automobile, oil refining, aircraft, and atomic energy plants.

The Ford Motor factory was a great pioneer in the field of automation. Let us pay a visit to the factory where engine blocks for Ford cars are made.

An engine block is made of heavy cast iron. It needs many holes and openings of different sizes. These holes must be exactly the right size and they must be perfectly smooth and even.

The Ford automatic machines move the two hundred pound engine blocks from one place to another. They turn them gently to the proper position. Each hole is drilled, smoothed, and carefully measured. If a measurement isn't perfect, the machine stops. It flashes a signal to a human worker to come and see what is wrong. But the work hasn't stopped in the meantime. The engine block has automatically been sent over to another drilling machine. There is no interruption in the work at all.

There used to be delays when drills or blades got dull. No one would realize this until the tools began to do poor work. Then the machine would flash its trouble light, and someone would come to check. Now, the storage unit of the computer has a record of how long each tool should last. Just *before* the tool gets dull a signal light flashes on the control panel. A worker stops the machine for a moment and replaces the worn part. Now no engine block must be thrown away because it was ruined by a dull tool.

This machine even cleans up after itself. All of the scrap metal which falls out after drilling or cutting is swept up. Then it is sent back to the steel mill to be melted down and used over again.

One automatic machine turns out an engine block every eighteen minutes, with the help of forty-eight workmen. It used to take four hundred workers forty minutes to make the same block!

While computer-operated machinery is a great help in ordinary factories, it isn't *necessary*. The factories *could* work without it, even though it would take much longer.

But this isn't true of the atomic energy industry. There probably wouldn't be any such industry without computers—no atomic power plants, no atomic ships, none of the wonderful peace-time uses of this kind of energy.

There are two reasons for this. First, much of the work needs such extremely careful control, that human workers could probably not do it. Second, when atoms are smashed, they give off deadly rays. No human being should be exposed to these rays. All of the work is done automatically. The humans remain safe behind thick walls. They watch what is happening on television screens.

In spite of great care, however, it sometimes happens that a worker picks up a bit of dangerous radioactive material on his shoes or clothing. It is much too small to see and he might never know it was there until he became seriously ill. To guard against this, anyone who

is ready to leave the building steps up to a special-purpose computer. Flashing lights show at once if there are
any dangerous specks on the person and exactly where
they are. They can then be removed. When the computer finds that all is well, a green light flashes.

In the atomic energy factory, the computer saves lives. In other kinds of factories, computers have set people free from boring, "slave" jobs. These people now do more interesting, better paying work. The machine has become the slave.

Large numbers of people have found jobs in the computer industry itself. Computers need designers, builders, servicemen, and programmers!

10

THE SKY'S THE LIMIT

We have seen that computers are of great use in science and industry. But there is no limit to the kinds of jobs they can do.

Computers suddenly came to everyone's attention on election night, back in 1952. Dwight D. Eisenhower and Adlai E. Stevenson were running for president. Naturally, people were eager to know who would win. Early in the evening, as the first votes began to come in, the figures were fed to a *Univac* computer. *Univac* was also given great batches of facts about other elections.

When only the first three million votes had been counted, *Univac* predicted that Eisenhower would win— in forty-three states with four hundred thirty-eight electoral votes. When the polls closed and every vote was counted, *Univac* was off by only four electoral votes!

And that isn't the only kind of prediction a computer can make. Once, a group of sports writers for the University of Pittsburgh were trying to predict the winner of a football game with Pennsylvania State University. They went over to the U. S. Steel building in Pittsburgh and asked permission to use the *IBM 650* computer.

The writers gave the machine information about the weight and speed of the players, what they did in past games, and even the number of years the coaches had been with the teams. The 650 whirled through its lightning math and said that probably each team would score once. Sure enough, the game ended in a 7-7 tie!

Computers help our government in taking the census, ordering supplies, and figuring taxes and social security.

One of the promising new uses of computers is in the field of medicine. Doctors have started to use computers to help find out what is wrong with a patient.

Sometimes a doctor examines a sick person and finds out many things about him. But he still doesn't know what disease the patient has. The disease may be one that is very rare in this country. Perhaps the doctor has never come across it before.

The doctor lists everything that he found in his examination of the patient, and feeds the information to a computer. The computer looks in its memory for a dis-

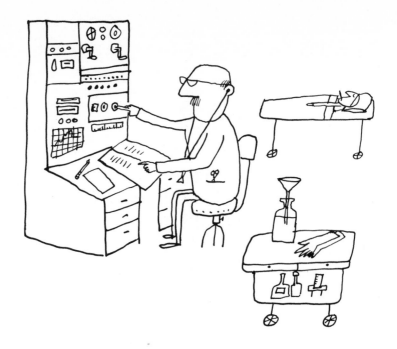

ease that exactly matches the patient's symptoms. The doctor gets a quick answer and can start the treatment right away. This speed can often save a life.

Computers have come into the world of literature, too. For centuries scholars have argued about whether a famous poem called the *Iliad* was really written by the ancient Greek, Homer. Some people thought that the long poem was written by more than one person.

James McDonough, a graduate student at Columbia University, decided to find out with the help of a computer. He prepared a punch card for each of the *Iliad's*

15,693 lines. The card showed the way in which the words and lines were arranged. The computer was programmed to count and make lists of all lines with the same word rhythm.

There were so many similar lines that Mr. McDonough decided that the *Iliad* **was** all written by the same man. It took four years of week-end work to do the study. It would have taken between twenty and forty years to do it without a computer!

There are computers that understand the human voice. There are computers that read business English. But most amazing of all, there are computers that translate foreign languages!

Whenever a scientist makes an important discovery, he writes an article about it—but naturally, in his own language. Sometimes a team of workers spends months, or even years, solving a scientific problem. When they are all finished they may find out that the same thing had been done before and printed in a journal. But they didn't know about it because the article was printed in Russian or Chinese.

There are not many scientists in our country who can read these languages. Just imagine how useful it is to have a translation machine that can read all of the scientific papers and translate them into English.

The first important experiment in this field was made at Georgetown University with an *IBM 701* computer. The machine was programmed with a Russian-English dictionary of about two hundred and fifty words, and six rules of grammar. Simple Russian sentences were fed into the machine. They came out printed in English! The English was not perfect, but it could be understood.

Since that experiment, there have been great improvements. There are now machines that can translate any one of four different languages into English.

Just think, perhaps some day all the peoples of the world will be able to understand each other—just by pressing buttons on a computer!

The *Arizona Journal,* a daily newspaper, was the first newspaper to purchase a computer to set type. The computer sets up the advertising sections, and handles the bookkeeping as well.

The Neiman-Marcus department store in Dallas, Texas, has bought a computer to help people pick out gifts. The shopper fills out a form which asks the sex and age of the person who will receive the gift. It also asks his occupation, hobbies, and how much the shopper wants to spend.

This information is punched on IBM cards and fed into the machine. The computer then prints a list of ten suitable gifts!

A New York high school has a computer which is used to train students in computer operation. When the students make a mistake the machine "swears" at them. One student failed to push a button when he was supposed to and the machine printed:

> *Please press my 6-bit button.*
> *The button is on the console.*
> *If you don't press my 6-bit button soon, I'll start swearing.*
> *%$#&'()"$%#&($& ** —+!4—$ About time.*
> *I can add, subtract, multiply or divide. What is your choice?*

The computer age has really just begun. It is hard to imagine all the things that computers will be able to do in years to come. And that word "imagine" is an important word. Every bit of scientific progress has been made because someone was able to *imagine*. And that is what a computer can't do.

Computers are clever because the men who made them are clever. Machines **do.** Men **think.**

GLOSSARY

address The letters or numbers (or both) that tell where a piece of information can be found in the *memory storage*.

bootstrap Instructions to a computer to put a section of a program into the *memory storage*.

bug Anything that keeps a computer from working properly. The trouble may be mechanical, electrical, or electronic. Or, it may be a mistake in the program.

cobol A computer language made up of standard business English. The word comes from *Common Business Oriented Language*.

coding (noun) A series of numbers or other symbols that are used in a program to tell a computer what to do.

de-bug	To correct anything that is wrong with a computer. See *bug*.
dump	To switch information from one part of a computer's memory to another part of the memory. Or, to send it to the *output*.
hardware	Any of a computer's parts.
leapfrog test	A special program which looks for errors in a computer's work.
nanosecond	A billionth of a second.
random access	A system of giving every piece of information its own address in the *memory unit*. There is no need to sort information that is to be stored. And you never have to look for anything that has been stored. You just have to know its address.
real-time	A computer system that works so fast that no time is lost. In rocket-tracking, for example, a *real-time* computer tells where the rocket is while it is still there.
remote sub-sets	Input and output units which may be far away from the main computer. The airline office agent-set is a *remote sub-set*.

software   Cards or tape containing a computer program.

solid-state   A type of computer in which current does not have to pass through space, as in vacuum tubes.

transistor   A very small electronic part that has replaced the vacuum tube. It is smaller, more reliable, and does not need to be air-conditioned. Transistors are used in solid-state computers.

INDEX

FEUILLET DE CIRCULATION
DATE DUE

(3-3-329)